A Kangaroo's World

written and illustrated by Caroline Arnold

PICTURE WINDOW BOOKS
Minneapolis, Minnesota

Special thanks to our advisers for their expertise:

Peter Courtney, Divisional Curator, Native Fauna
Melbourne Zoo, Parkville, Victoria, Australia

Susan Kesselring, M.A., Literacy Educator
Rosemount–Apple Valley–Eagan (Minnesota) School District

Editor: Christianne Jones
Designer: Hilary Wacholz
Page Production: Michelle Biedscheid
Art Director: Nathan Gassman
The illustrations in this book were created with cut paper.

Picture Window Books
5115 Excelsior Boulevard
Suite 232
Minneapolis, MN 55416
877-845-8392
www.picturewindowbooks.com

Printed in the United States of America.

 All books published by Picture Window Books
are manufactured with paper containing at least
10 percent post-consumer waste.

Library of Congress Cataloging-in-Publication Data
Arnold, Caroline.
A kangaroo's world / written and illustrated by
Caroline Arnold.
p. cm. — (Caroline Arnold's animals)
Includes index.
ISBN-13: 978-1-4048-3983-0 (library binding)
1. Kangaroos—Juvenile literature. I. Title.
QL737.M35A733 2008
599.2'22—dc22   2007032894

There are more than 50 species in the kangaroo family. This book is about eastern gray kangaroos.

Where they live: Australia

Habitat: grasslands and open woodlands

Food: grass, shrubs, and leaves

Height: 5 to 6 feet (1.5 to 1.8 meters)

Weight: 72 to 154 pounds (32 to 69 kilograms)

Animal class: mammals

Scientific name: *Macropus giganteus*

Kangaroos are marsupials. A female marsupial has a special pouch where her baby is carried and fed. Her baby is called a joey. Hop along with a kangaroo joey and learn about a kangaroo's world.

Snip, snip. At the edge of an Australian woodland, kangaroos nibble grass. They cut off the tough blades and chew them to bits.

4

One of the female kangaroos stops eating. She leans over and licks her pouch. She is getting it ready for her new baby. It will be born soon.

Kangaroos live in groups called mobs. Between two and 30 kangaroos may live in one mob.

The baby kangaroo has just been born. He has no hair and cannot hear or see. The tiny baby grabs his mother's fur and pulls his way along her belly. The baby uses his sense of smell to find his mother's pouch.

Inside the pouch, he drinks milk. The baby kangaroo will stay in the pouch for many months.

At birth, a kangaroo baby is no bigger than a jelly bean. It weighs about .04 ounce (1 gram).

At 6 months, a baby kangaroo is about the size of a house cat. It weighs about 4.5 pounds (2 kg).

At 6 months, the baby kangaroo's eyes are open and his fur has started to grow. His floppy ears fall over his face.

The baby kangaroo sticks his head out of the pouch for the first time. He sees other kangaroos eating and resting. Far away, an emu runs across the plain. A flock of galahs squawk overhead. The noise startles him, and he ducks back into the pouch.

When the young kangaroo is 8 months old, he is ready to come out of the pouch. He leans forward and slips onto the ground. He stands up on his two big feet, using his tail for balance.

At first, the kangaroo stays close to his mother. When he gets tired, he dives back into the pouch. He lets his mother do the hopping.

A kangaroo jumps into the pouch headfirst. Then it somersaults to turn itself around.

11

The young kangaroo is now old enough to eat grass. He bites it off, chews it, and swallows it. Then he coughs it up and chews it again. This makes the grass easier to digest. When the kangaroo is thirsty, he pokes his head into his mother's pouch and drinks some milk.

Kangaroos get most of the water they need from their food.

As the kangaroos move about, they watch and listen for danger. Wild dogs, called dingoes, and other animals sometimes hunt kangaroos.

Suddenly, one of the kangaroos spots a dingo. The kangaroo pounds his feet against the ground. *Thump! Thump! Thump!*

dingo

wedge-tailed eagle

The young kangaroos dive into their mothers' pouches.
Then, with giant leaps, all of the kangaroos bound
across the plain. Soon they are far away and safe.

Foxes, eagles, and dingoes are the
main predators of kangaroos.

The kangaroos look for shady places to rest when it is hot. Sometimes they dig shallow holes in the ground. They lie in the cool, damp earth.

In winter, the kangaroos' soft fur keeps them warm. During the summer, the kangaroos pant and sweat to keep cool. They lick their arms, and as their skin dries, they cool down.

Kangaroos clean themselves by licking and scratching.

sulphur-crested cockatoo

The young kangaroo likes to play with other young kangaroos in the mob. They stand up tall and punch with their paws. During these play fights, they do not hurt each other. Only adult male kangaroos have real fights. The strongest ones become the leaders of the mob.

When a kangaroo kicks, the long, sharp nails on its center toes can make a painful gash.

When the young kangaroo is 1 year old, his mother has a new baby. In a few months, that baby will be big enough to come out of the pouch. Then it will be time for the older kangaroo to be on his own.

He will be nearly full grown and able to care for himself.
He will leave the mob and find another group of kangaroos.
One day he may be strong enough to become the leader of
his own mob.

Where do kangaroos live?

Members of the kangaroo family are found in Australia, New Guinea, Indonesia, and neighboring islands. The eastern gray kangaroo lives in coastal areas of eastern and southeastern Australia and in Tasmania. The closely related western gray kangaroo is found in western and southern Australia. Gray kangaroos are the second largest kangaroo species. The largest are the red kangaroos. They live in the dry interior regions of Australia.

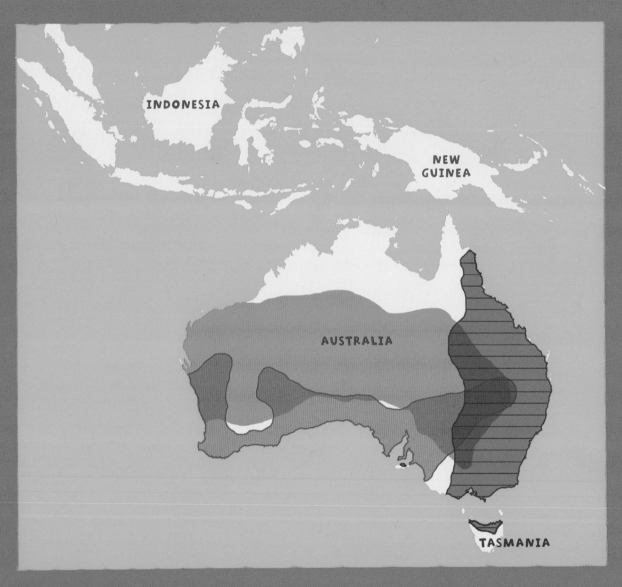

RED KANGAROO   WESTERN GRAY KANGAROO   EASTERN GRAY KANGAROO

Kangaroo Fun Facts

Giant Leapers

An adult gray kangaroo can jump 30 feet (9 m) in a single bound and leap over a fence 9 feet (2.7 m) high. Its long, heavy tail keeps it from tipping forward as it hops.

Fast Hoppers

A kangaroo can hop long distances without tiring. It moves at about 11 miles (18 km) per hour, but it can travel at speeds of up to 40 miles (64 km) per hour for short distances.

Long Tails

The tail of an eastern gray kangaroo is 4 feet (1.2 m) long. When the kangaroo sits, the tail becomes a sturdy support.

Big Feet

The scientific name for kangaroos means "big foot." The hind feet of an eastern gray kangaroo are 18 inches (46 cm) long.

Cud Chewers

Like cattle and sheep, kangaroos cough up their food and chew it as cud. This helps them digest tough plants.

Long Lives

In the wild, gray kangaroos live for 6 to 8 years. In zoos, they can live to be 20 years old.

Glossary

cud—half-eaten food that an animal burps up and chews again

digest—to break down food so it can be used by the body

dingo—a wild dog that lives in Australia

emu—large, flightless Australian bird related to the ostrich

galah—Australian bird, also called the pink breasted cockatoo

habitat—the place or natural conditions in which a plant or animal lives

joey—a baby marsupial

mammal—a warm-blooded animal that feeds its babies milk

marsupial—animal whose babies are carried in a pouch in the mother's body

mob—a group of kangaroos

plain—a large area of flat land with few large plants

predator—an animal that hunts and eats other animals

To Learn More

More Books to Read

Hewett, Joan. *A Kangaroo Joey Grows Up.* Carolrhoda Books, 2002.

Markle, Sandra. *Outside and Inside Kangaroos.* New York: Atheneum, 1999.

Noonan, Diana. *The Kangaroo.* Philadelphia: Clubhouse Books, 2003.

On the Web

FactHound offers a safe, fun way to find Web sites related to topics in this book. All of the sites on FactHound have been researched by our staff.

1. Visit www.facthound.com

2. Type in this special code: 1404839836

3. Click on the FETCH IT button.

Your trusty FactHound will fetch the best sites for you!

Index

Look for all of the books in Caroline Arnold's Animals series:

A Kangaroo's World
A Killer Whale's World
A Koala's World
A Panda's World
A Penguin's World
A Platypus' World
A Wombat's World
A Zebra's World